THE JANET AND JOHN BOOKS: OFF TO PLAY

 Contender Merchandising is a division of the Contender
Entertainment Group www.contendergroup.com

Janet and John © Contender Ltd 2007

First published in 1949

This edition published in 2007 by Summersdale Publishers Ltd.

Summersdale Publishers Ltd
46 West Street
Chichester
West Sussex
PO19 1RP
UK

www.summersdale.com

Printed and bound in China

ISBN 13: 978-1-84024-615-5

OFF TO PLAY

BY

M<small>ABEL</small> O'D<small>ONNELL</small> <small>AND</small> R<small>ONA</small> M<small>UNRO</small>

ILLUSTRATED BY

F<small>LORENCE</small> <small>AND</small> M<small>ARGARET</small> H<small>OOPES</small>

summersdale

This is Janet.

This is John.

This is Mother.

This is Father.

See Janet, Mother.
See Janet play.

This is Father.

See John and Father.

See the dog, Janet.

See the little dog.

Come, little dog.

Come to Janet.

See the little dog come.

Run, little dog, run.

Look at the little dog.

The little dog can run fast.

The little dog can jump.

Jump, little dog, jump.

Mother, look at my little dog.

I like to skip.

I like to skip and jump.

I can skip fast.

Here I come.

Run fast, little dog.

See the kittens.
One little,
Two little,
Three little kittens.
One, two, three.

John, see my kitten play.

My kitten can play.

One, two, three kittens.

One little kitten can play.

Look, Janet.

Look at the basket.

One kitten runs to the basket.

Jump in, kitten.

Jump in and play.

One, two, three,

Three little kittens.

Three kittens in a basket.

The kittens play in the basket.

Look at the boats.

Big boats and little boats.

This is my little red boat.

I like big boats, John.
Look at the big red boat.
I want to go in it.

See John in the boat.

John is in the big boat.

Let me come, John.

Come in, Janet.

Come in and play.

Let us play in the big boat.

John, see the aeroplanes.
One, two, three aeroplanes.
I can see three aeroplanes.

Look at the aeroplane.

See it go up.

See the aeroplane fly.

It can fly very fast.

Fly fast, big aeroplane.

Janet said,

"Look at the aeroplane.

I want to fly in it."

John said,

"Look, Janet, look.

See the aeroplane come down."

John said,
"I see the red slide.
I want to go on the slide."

John went up to the top.

"Here I go," said John.

"See me go up to the top."

John went down the slide.

John went down fast.

"See me come down," said John.

"Go up, Janet.

You can slide too.

Go up the big red slide.

Go up to the top."

Janet went up the slide.

John said,
"See me go up the slide.
I like to go to the top.
I can go up very fast.
Here I come."

Janet said,
"I like to go down.
I go down very fast.
See me go down, John."

Janet said,

"Look at the horses, John.

Let us ride.

Come on, John.

Let us ride on the horses."

Here I come, Janet.

Here I come.

I want a ride too.

I want a ride on a horse.

Mother said,
"You may ride a horse, John.
Jump on, Janet.
You may ride too."

Look, Mother.

Look at my horse.

It can go up and down.

Up and down I go.

See me ride.

I like my horse.

It can go up and down too.

My horse can go fast.

Here I come, Mother.

Thank you for the ride.

My horse went up and down.

My horse went very fast.

Thank you, little horse.

Thank you for the ride.

Good-bye, little horse, good-bye.

Good-bye!
Good-bye!

VOCABULARY

The 32 new words introduced in *Off to Play* appear in the following order :–

2. This	16. basket	27. top
is	in	went
3.	17. a	28.
4. Mother	18. big	29. you
5. Father	red	too
6.	19. it	30.
7.	want	31.
8.	20. let	32.
9. to	me	33.
10. at	21. us	34. may
fast	22.	35.
11.	23. fly	36.
12. like	very	37. thank
skip	24. said	for
13.	25.	38. good-bye
14.	26. slide	39.
15.	on	

WORD LIST

The following 59 words are used in *Off to Play*. Of these 59 words, 27 (printed in *italics*) have already been introduced in *Here We Go*.

a	*I*	red
aeroplane	in	*ride*
and	is	*run*
at	it	
		said
basket	*Janet*	*see*
big	*John*	skip
boat	*jump*	slide
can	*kitten*	thank
come		*the*
	let	this
dog	like	*three*
down	*little*	to
	look	too
fast		top
Father	may	*two*
fly	me	
for	Mother	*up*
	my	us
go		
good-bye	on	very
	one	
here		want
horse	*play*	went
		you